Hearts & Farts

By Ryan Marcel
(Buynak)

I was gonna call this book
"Farts & Hearts"

But figured that was a stupid name,
so I changed it…

to "Hearts & Farts."

Aka: Love & Laughter

Because that is all that matters.

You're welcome.

-

No part of this book may be reproduced without expressed, written consent or permission of the author or publishing entities, except for brief quotes for press or review purposes.

Hearts & Farts
All content copyright 2023 © Ryan Buynak
Published by Coyote Blood Press
Always in association with Paradisiac Publishing

ISBN: 9798388636188

Cover Photo by Keren Buynak

Cover Design by Enid Casablanca
www.rawmade.co

Follow Ryan Buynak on Instagram: @coyoteblood

Previous works by Ryan Buynak:

- Yo Quiero Mas Sangre: Random Acts of Poetry
- The Ghost of the Wooden Squid: Random Acts of Poetry
- Montreal on October
- Future Underwater Tomahawk: Random Acts of Poetry
- Sleeping: I'm Just Not Good At It
- Sleeping 2: I'm Still Just Not Good At It
- Writer, Bartender, Skateboarder
- Stolen Days in LA
- Pistol Pantomimes
- Coyote Blood Will Kill/Love You
- A Whole Bag of Hammers

Dedicated to my Daughter

Be Brave!

Think Positive!

#thelittlethingsarethebigthings

All you need is hope
The size of your pinky toe or a pea
To see that life is for living…

Putting away the dishes,
The sun coming through the kitchen window,
Motes of dust being kicked up,
As I sip coffee and snack on bacon.

Upstairs, my daughter is singing,
And I text my pals
About how lucky I am.

Poem

I am not punk enough.
I am not hipster enough.
I am not hip-hop on the surface.
I hide poetry in my pockets.
I am man enough to man-up.

Saponify

A kiss, a cup of confidence,
a cardigan, and you can
call my morning Sunshine.

An imperfect plot
to pin down my soul
prior to noon, and you can
call it all a success.

A noose without a knot,
with a nip of tea,
a nice knee on my neck,
a new book, and you can
call my night Revelry.

The future without fear,
the visions clear, and you can
call my dreams…Reality.

The Opposite of Solipsism

post office and podiatrist,
Hobby Lobby and Home Depot,
nothing a comedy podcast can't handle.

I want to write about regular people
doing regular things like doing the dishes,
debating sell-by dates on food,
worrying, forgetting, worrying, remembering,
loving.

we are all fucked up
in big and little ways,
and it is easy to write about trauma,
but it is hard to write about dining room silence,
or crayon box distance.

we are all doing our best,
complete with idiosyncratic routine,
milestones and mediocre days,
doesn't mean it doesn't matter.

Lifting Light Tonight

gonna read one poem tonight, but write 22, and if my voice shakes when I read it aloud it's because I'm just a bunch of energy and bones inside a nervous system, trying to flow. it's tough looking at yourself, because you never like what you see. no one does. what order is your Zoom? where am I in your life? and the questions come, as they always do, in the decaying evening, after a long day, balancing bullshit and business. when will I have my first heart attack? I am tired and I want a simple life without heavy questions. light, like why doesn't Taco Bell have chips and salsa?

we, excursion

hardly a soup slurps
barely a bozo burps
than a cactus catches
a cat's dress and pulls
it into a wretched mess.

the light in the cuss
lends itself to us
as a beacon between
doldrums and dreams
where seamless days
come and leave.

where our hearts are
broken as sparrow bones
in summer camp starts where
the ranks of the expired orange
is worse than the light.

Anxiety

Pretty fucked up that my body,
a chemistry lab of meat,
simply chooses to make me feel
a little bit nervous sometimes for no reason.

Nose Hairs, but on the outside

Getting old is weird.

I used to stand on the subway
and stare into old men's ears,
marveling at the amount of hair
coming out of there.

Just as well,
I am always amazed
how old dudes either don't see
or don't give a shit
about their fern forest of nose hairs
poking out, impossible to ignore.

People can grow hair almost anywhere,
including the surface of the nose,
and that is where my age is showing,
not counting wrinkles
and gray pubes, of course.

Terminal hair is more noticeable
than vellus hair,
because it's often dark and thick,
and on the nose
terminal hairs may cluster on the tip.

And so now part of my life
is playing with these hairs,
until they are long or insufferable enough
to where I walk upstairs
and pull them out with tweezers.

Poem

today Franco assured me
that one day I will make it,
one day I will have my own Wikipedia page,
he said, and I had to laugh,
because if that is the barometer of success
he sees in me then I know
I can do a little bit better than that.

pensée scarper in the frondescence

you know that melodramatic Macbeth
soliloquy at the end of the play?
the whole "Life is but...a poor player
that struts and frets his hour upon the stage"
and "a tale told by an idiot...signifying nothing?"

I've always loved Shakespeare but now...
I feel it in my bones, especially Macbeth,
and Hamlet, and Measure for Measure
has always been there but now I see it
in a new cyclical air of change.

there are no isolated moments,
we are in a closed fist,
and that is why I write
poems of the self, the body, pasta,
the city and—always, above all—love.

the world does change and us in it,
thus we stay the same, signifying nothing,
and because of that, we are everything,
rich and revered by renowned humans
for being smart enough to be simple.

never stop moving, strutting upon the stage,
because you are more than just a tale
told by idiots around a fire or a foundry,
who think themselves to be more than themselves,
because now I know who I am and where I fit in.

8
(*Thanks, Dr. Becky*)

Eight-year-olds can be stubborn
and defiant,
slamming doors and rolling eyes,
in their attempts to establish
their independence and individuality.

Acting like doing their chores
is an act of torture is common,
and straight-up ignoring their parents
is an 8-year-old hallmark.

Eight can be patience-trying
and headache-inducing,
but after a particularly rough day
or a huge meltdown,
they still just want a hug.

It's hard parenting an 8-year-old,
but it's hard being an 8-year-old, too,
so when possible, choose compassion
when your 8-year-old is acting like…
an 8-year-old!

St. Augustine of Hippo

traipsing through life,
marking milestones
with smiles and frowns,
addresses and towns
with blues and tattoos.

from bars to scars,
the world is a book
and you must read many pages.

having recently taken my daughter
to Disney and her first NBA game,
today, as I hit official middle age,
all I want is a regular day:
workout, work, tons of coffee, and mooches.

I wouldn't mind
if I found five bucks on the sidewalk,
or if I saw a douchebag wearing polo-over-polo,
or if a beautiful woman hit on me,
but I also wouldn't mind a forgettable day of *nada*.

Poem

I sit here
reading
a book
called
Also a Poet

And wonder
if my daughter
will ever
write
about me

For now
it is my turn
to write
about
her.

P.S. I am a scorpio.

it's weird being the same age as old people.
Poem
poem
poem
poem
stuff
life.
I wanna be a mystery.
other stuff.
poem.
life.
but I am probably a comedy.
it's 2023, so can't I identify as anything I want?
in that case, I want to be…
I don't know what I want to be.
only what I don't want to be.
I don't want to be me all the time.
sometimes I need a fucking break.
today I identify as a boring bro.
tomorrow I will be a lazy freak.
other stuff.
poem.
life.
me.
Always.
But not forever.

No Puns on the Weekend

Every Saturday I sleep in
and forget how it is,
just how it is.

I wake and read Chen Chen,
at least for today,
I watch Jules and Jim,
that's just how it is.

I think about
my high school gym
for some reason,
that's just how it is.

Not checking work emails,
not writing poems,
just how it is.

Inside jokes are important.

Football Sucks

Love baseball,
but I don't know it
as much as I know basketball.

I don't know shit
about Football,
other than it is slow and boring.

To me, teams should
go both ways,
and not wear helmets.

just two pots and a wooden spoon, dirtied in the process

making penne ala vodka
in the kitchen
reminds me of my early days
in an NYC kitchen
making penne ala vodka
with Mary and Keren.

before kids,
before big mistakes,
before life kicked us in the shins
yet inspired us to smile, still.

despite its simplicity,
vodka sauce projects an allure
that a basic marinara simply does not;
add in a dash of nostalgia
and I can't get enough.

despite its simplicity,
life is complicated
and basic poems
do not encapsulate it,
and I wish I could go back
for seconds.

when I am eating carbs,
it is a staple;
when I am sad,
it is a must;
with a Tokyo Police Club soundtrack,
and a dessert of cookies
(from the bodega).

Headline: Parkland Problems

Raspberries at Heron Bay Publix
are better than the Raspberries at the "fancy" Publix!

Man in perpetual pajama pant
makes woman in Lululemon leggings sign his petition
to require pizza delivery style signs
on top of all resident automobiles.

Frog gets stuck and dies in homeowners AC unit;
homeowner rips off frog's head trying to remove it.

Tennis rained out.

Long Cove pool is too cold at 88°
in dead of August summer.

Local woman's Peloton machine insists
she wear a Peloton branded shirt
when she goes to pick up her child from school.

Heron Heights is better than Park Trails!

Tennis back on.

Valentine's Day banned in town
because it is also anniversary of school shooting.

Raccoon only scavenging for organic trash,
including cauliflower side cans and gluten-free garbage

Turns out nerdy Jewish dad everyone thought was 55 years
old is actually only 35 but due to baldness and terrible dress
sense everyone assumed he was older.

Local photographer won't shut up about NFTs.

Salad place closes; açaí place opens!

Golf carts: pandemic menace or mid life crisis?

Woman with RBF actual bitch.

Garbage man doesn't take cardboard box filled with other cardboard boxes even though it was leaning against the recycling bin.

Mold on raspberries found at other Publix in next town.

Local Teen claims to know the Island Boys, says they are "chill AF," whatever that means.

Dinosaurs everywhere, no one bats an eye.

Eleven months of summer but everyone pretends it's "not that bad today."

Driving sucks?

Fact: Area more expensive than Manhattan but everyone secretly denies it.

Açaí place closes; FroYo places opens!

Evidence shows no one is "living the dream" despite saying it as response to when others ask 'how are you?'

Ode to Budd Friedman

The man who built an empire of comedy clubs, dies at 90.
Starting with the original Improv in Midtown Manhattan,
he gave countless comedians a launching pad to fame,
but he also gave me my whole world, my whole worth,
because without the Orlando Improv, I would not have
the loves of my life, best friend and brother-in-law.
He gave Jay Leno his start, but he gave me my whole heart.
Budd's influence on live stand-up comedy is immeasurable,
but his effect on my life (and my child's existence) is
invaluable.

Sometimes Copywriter

Oh hey...So you're an eCom copywriter tryin' to be more better-er...Truckin' along with Header/Subheader/CTA ayy.What's this? [PLAIN TEXT]An eDuCaTiOn highlight?"Uh oh." <-- You, problyThey want to cover the acteyl-factor xf4 and how it blends with lavender molecules for skin that glows on World Tsunami day?Oh, and they have a sale...It's 20% off at 9:59 EST, 15% off at 10:59 EST, and 10.5% off at 11:59 and 33 seconds EST.And it's for 3 other products they'd like to eDuCatE the reader on.Plus, they also want to push to a blog post.It's about "The 3 Reasons Why This Blog Post Has Nothing To Do With This Email."And you're like. "Sir, this is a Wendy's."You with me?So, is there a secret method to knock out this madness lickity splickity?A proven formula so easy your uncle who stills uses a flip phone could do it?I dunno. Maybe?And so I was locked me in a closet until I cracked asked me to cover some email stuff that I find useful when... ya know... I'm writin' emails 'n stuff.

I am always trying to leave me alone

Oh, October Monday,
where art thou in my life
of leaving and left
me to be me?

Is this the day
I get it all right,
and say
tonight will be blessedly easy?

Is this the moment
it all gets whisked away
in a dizzy death
of the soul going bye-bye?

Oh, October noon,
no matter what goes down,
I am here, now, existing
in space and time, love and poetry.

fair assumption

Miami is a far car crash town.
where hurricanes happen.
and differences are abundant.
but similarities are a fairer assumption:

we all have socks in common.
everyone has ambition.
misguided or magnificent.

this place is worse than LA.
with fakes and flakes.
but it does have rhythm.
it's just hidden.

behind the white girls.
who are living their best Miami life.
and in front of the ghettos which are grand and scary.

chomping at the bits.
to get back to a real city.
because this one is sprawl.
and it will be underwater in 20 years.

The two types of phone users

When you put your phone on the table, say,
when you're having lunch with your friends,
do you place it screen facing up or down?

Your choice says a lot about you.

There are two main categories of people:
screen-facing-up people and screen-facing-down people.
Screen-facing-up people allow themselves—
more than screen-facing-down people—
to be interrupted by a call, text
or sudden need to check the weather or stock market.

Screen-facing-up people are open to being distracted
by anything that promises to be more interesting
than the friends they're physically with at the moment.

There are definitely more categories
of people than just these two
(e.g. phone-in-the-pocket, phone-in-the-bag,
phone-on-silent-mode,
phone-with-super-obnoxious-and-loud-ringtone),
but the idea is similar.

There's a wide spectrum of how committed you are
to being present, both mentally and physically, with people.

Depending on who you're with,
you move along this spectrum,
but at some level, we know we ought to prioritize
the people we're physically with.

When you put your phone on the table screen facing down,

it's a symbolic act: You're "turning down" the distractions.
You're "turning down" your need to be continually entertained.
You're "turning down" self-gratification.

Let's make the daily choice to be
screen-facing-down people,
because it's really the choice to show people
that they matter.

Mixed Greens

I want one documentary
about a normal dude,
who works in IT,
lives in the suburbs,
throws out an expired bag of mixed greens
without even opening it,
goes to therapy,
but at the end of the documentary
you find out he didn't have to.

You'll (dis)like this...

I remember when I was in high school, I was dating this college chick (BRAG!). So she lived in Gainesville and I was in high school in Orlando which is like 2 hours apart (long distance...definitely worked out). This was like 1999 and I remember telling someone (this fat chick named Sara without the H) that there should be a way for me to, like, chat with my long-distance-college-girlfriend through video —like see her face in real time—and she was like you stupid sonofabitch that will never be a thing. And at the moment, I did, I felt stupid.

Well, I hope Sara is somewhere thinking about that moment as much as I have. I hope she is on another stage somewhere else saying her side of this tale; that it was her who was stupid and she feels bad for talking shit to some co-worker in 1999. She definitely isn't doing that (despite what some people aka ladies are saying in their heads: well, she might, ya never know), and I hope she is dead...or divorced. Oh, don't worry. Me wishing that doesn't mean a thing because wishes aren't real, but if they were and I was the only one with the power to make wishes real then I would be God...maybe...but I wouldn't be here. Could you imagine? Being able to make a wish to yourself that comes true, but all you wished for was to be doing shitty storytelling and making people die!

You know what else is made up? Astrology. Zodiac shit. Now hear me out, the stars and the universe may play a bigger role in who we are, I don't know. Maybe, if you were born in Spring, you could have different traits than someone born in fall (which is way better...Scorpios!), but I refuse to believe some thick chick named Stefanie with an F with white dreads and tiny shoes in Brooklyn (or Austin or

Portland or Westwood) knows all about the energy of stars from a book she bought at Barnes and Noble. Now I know what you're saying: He is such a scorpio…he is passionate and blah blah blah, but you are wrong because I am a Libra, and I am sure some of you in here thought to yourself "I knew he was a Libra all along" but you would be wrong too because I am in fact a Pisces. It's all bullshit. Half the people who believe in crystals don't believe in Jesus and half the people who use essential oils also have Jesus fish decals on their Law and Order SUVs. Also, what is the deal with the fish? First Jesus was a lamb and then he was a fish on your Honda Pilot?

Lost in living the dream and now FaceTime exists.

HBO

The start of any HBO program
will always make me think of a couple specific things,
allowing my mind to time travel.

One of those things is
the show Entourage,
because at a certain period
all I had was a giant desktop HP, a futon,
and the first season of Entourage on DVD.

Another thing is
the thrill of having cable
as a child and what the static intro
meant to a poor kid such as myself.

And now that I think about it,
there was a stupid joke going around
when I was in elementary school,
where one kid would ask another
if he or she had HBO,
and if the other said yes,
they laughed and said Heavy Body Odor?

I am gonna go turn on HBOmax
(now just called MAX)
and watch a Rated R movie, like The Last Boy Scout.

Lil' Victories

it's okay to be grateful for some things
at the same time you are angry at others.

we live in one body, with infinite emotions.
I'm just a bunch of energy and bones inside a nervous
system, trying to flow.

after a life (40 fucking years) of little losses,
I could use a simple win, now and then.

it's tough looking at yourself,
because you never like what you see.

the set-up is life.
the punchline is time.

a couple big victories can
outweigh a lot of little losses,
and love can neutralize it all to nothing.

LA poem

I had left my recycled bag
of bastard poems at Beyond Baroque,
last night, before I got lost.

I took a cab back to Venice,
but the theater was closed.

I walked around to the back,
trying to find someone on the morning shift,
but all I found were garbage cans.

On top of one of the heaps was a plastic bag,
dew-wet and standing out.

Inside were my damp poems,
a box cutter,
and a half-filled Diet Dr. Pepper.

Poem

Last night, I felt pretty lonely on stage tbh. It feels like you have to always amplify your successes on social media, and that's why it's such a phony place to be sometimes. Artists don't talk about the shows that are difficult as much as they talk about the shows that are "sick."

When you're on your own on a big stage, singing about your bloody feelings, supporting a musical legend you know everyone is waiting patiently for, competing with air con / dry ice / people talking at the back like you can't hear everything in the room / the bar staff smashing glasses, it can be a pretty lonely place.

Gary Cooper

It just occurred to me.
I want that.

"The strong silent type. Ya know."

Just cool. Laid.
Back.

Time Traveling at the CVS on 27th & Park, but not for the reason you'd assume

The Replacements come on
over the speakers at this CVS,
and I time travel on the deodorant aisle,
Paul's voice taking me back
to another life when
I had just moved to NYC
and I was not even 25,
but feeling the most alive,
until now…

Ad

"In societies where modern conditions of production prevail, all of life presents itself as an immense accumulation of spectacles. Everything that was directly lived has moved away into representation."
- Guy Debord, Society of the Spectacle

So there I was, first day back,
back home, back in NYC,
my favorite place in the wide world,
and my feet were already killing me—
so much so that
I had subconsciously started walking different
and then my knee began to hurt,
which was new and worse than the plantar.

I took a break in Brooklyn,
to lean against a pole—
telephone wire sneakers dangling above—
and that's when I saw
the crude, Xerox-looking paper flyer
taped to the thing, asking "Need Support?"
with cut tabs that said: Yes, shoessuck.com.

Life is a funny sunset
(or we live in the Matrix),
because that paper tab led me to Fulton,
and now as I am about to buy a pair
I wanted to celebrate the universe
in hopes that it will further reward me (my feet)
with insoles that actually do the trick,
because I refuse to wear ugly dad shoes
and manifesting seems to be working lately
(i.e. Ron Perlman).

Love is a gateway drug.

Poem

Loneliness isn't so bad.
Try to embrace it when you can.

Show your scars
(Your marks are remarkable…
and you should bloody love them.)

Some scars manifest physically, others emotionally.
Some might be barely visible,
other's worn like a hi-vis/hi-res, bold and bright badge.
Some might have lingered in your life for decades now,
fading gently into the background.
Other's might be fresh, open, exposed wounds, still bleeding
through that Teletubbies plaster you pasted onto it
a few lifetimes ago.
Some are tattoos that define you
and some are regrets in the form
of a Ghostbusters logo on your butt
from one night when you were drunk in Harlem.

Whatever the case, wherever they're from,
however you might have acquired them —
do not look at them in disgust.
Don't look down at them, don't cover them up,
conceal them, hide them away.
What might sometimes seem broken
is actually just art, showcased in a newer form.
Like a mosaic, fragments and scraps and shards
sequenced in such a way that a masterpiece is born.
On their own, you might think that they're the remnants
of something that was once whole.
But when you piece them together,
hold them up to the sunlight, take a step back just to admire
— they glitter, they sparkle, they shine.
They make something so much bigger,
so much brighter, so much braver.
They fit together so flawlessly, because
they're bits and pieces of you.

a wilting sunflower seems so sad

Forgetting is the saddest thing in the world to me.
Forgotten love, forgotten hate, forgotten passion.

I truly wish I could remember everything,
like flashing neon, like dirty pizza-rat graffiti.

My life, my work, is just an attempt to brand my existence
in order to somehow live forever, not be forgotten,
and never forget.

I want to take a snapshot of it all and my life amongst it.
I want to travel back in time to specific moments.

From the neon in Times Sq.
to the stickers on my childhood bedroom door,
I am overwhelmed by all of me, but I still want to keep it.

raincoats are made to be abused...unlike my heart

water and weather,
waiting in the back of the closet
until you remember,
my love is not a rain slicker,
so don't pull me out, dust me off,
when the tide turns away
from your flood of forever.

Pleasant Nothing

the cardinals come visit me
while I read my book in the garden.

the Georgia afternoon has shifted
from hot rain to cool overcast breeze,
which allows me to sit outside
and finish this book.

these days of doing nothing
have become my favorite thing,
especially with six jobs, a podcast,
constant travel up and down the east coast,
and being a dad.

the bees buzz my head
on their way to and from the flowers,
while I dog-ear the page
and pay attention
to the wonders of the small world.

I am happy to be small, insignificant,
but part of the whole parade of days.

Doom Boy

I am a writer of little acclaim,
a troublemaker of mild renown,
and a corporeal mass of about 190lbs.

The way I got here was that in every single choice
I was presented with in life,
I took the path that seemed more adventurous
but was actually very stupid.

My mission is doom,
but then again that is the mission of all of us,
whether we push for it or not;
I am just having fun with it.

I am still a boy
in the body of an aging man,
doing the best that I can,
sometimes succeeding, other times not.

Let's Get Old

everything makes more sense.
and my confidence is coming back.
sure, my feet hurt.
but, darling, my heart is healing.

I'm an acolyte of life.
and I can build a wobbly table.
but I have to get out of Florida.
because I am short on time.

we could fly to Israel.
make love on the stairs.
cut like a dull knife.
write like a dull pencil.

I am hungry for Heaven.
starving for Hell.
wish you were with me.
got a fever to tell.

gray mustache.
golden afternoons.
no more blues.
never not you.

No Hat

Feeling my messy hair today.
It's the right amount of sleep dirty.
Not greasy, just floppy.
And it's just asking for a woman.
To run her fingers through it.

One day I will buy you that bench

Established in 1986,
the Adopt-A-Bench program provides funding to maintain
and endow the care of Central Park's
more than 10,000 benches
and their surrounding landscapes.

To date, more than 7,000 benches have been adopted.

A bench is a wonderful way to memorialize
or honor a loved one, or share as a meaningful gift
for a birthday, anniversary, new baby, or graduation.

In recognition of contributions to the fund,
the Conservancy will install a personalized plaque
on a Park bench of the donor's choosing.

Benches may be endowed for $10,000,
but legacy is priceless.

"What if a sadistic desert chicken had legit trompe-l'œil skills and access to dynamite?"

before humans have the ability to talk,
how do we articulate inner thoughts,
is it all just images and instincts?

my least favorite part of life
is waiting for people to get off the plane.

time travel exists but it's only in the form of poetry,
WHadmin vs W.H. Auden,
welcome to the accepted future.

warm, freshly-baked chocolate chip cookies
are my favorite part of life.

playing time against my troubles
as I run into rain and break,
I would love to run the NYC marathon,
but will never train for it.

I am tired so I drank coffee,
but it skipped the energy
and just made me jittery (but I am still tired).

you ever wonder why days are long
but life is short?

we have no bread,
only circuses.

Bug on the Basketball Court

I don't know how much value
I have in this universe,
but as I run back and forth,
up and down the basketball court,
I notice a pretty little green bug
carefully and slowly crossing it
like a vast concrete desert.

It is definitely going to get stepped on
by one of these old dudes
who don't care about the birds
that fly above or the bugs
that crawl below their outlet sneakers.

Florida is full of bugs and old men,
and while I can't save them all or any,
I stop mid-court to pick this one up
and walk it over to the grass,
much to the chagrin of the guys
who take this Sunday "Man League"
much too seriously as if it mattered,
as if the love of their children
was dependent on them winning
a pick-up game in a park.

I don't know how much value
I have in this universe,
but I know it is worth more
than a three-pointer and a couple rebounds,
yet maybe I am just a bug
on a bigger basketball court,
needing to be saved.

a Strategy for Getting Out of the Darkness (It's Not What You Might Think)

last night I dreamed
of a beautiful woman
and now I have a crush
on nothing.

love is a good-time gallow
but I'm pretty good at forgiving,
the brightest light that shines
makes you squint and look away.

the best strategy
for getting out of the darkness
is just following the shadows
until you come to the sun that casts them.

everything beautiful
isn't real,
and everything real
is *unobtainium*.

make it luminous,
set it ablaze,
achieve by trying,
live by dying.

the only way to see the light
is to get through darkness,
head-on with eyes open,
a little love in Autumn.

last night I dreamed
of yesterday

and tomorrow,
but today is all that matters.

Poetry is a Laxative

Shitting on life.
Shitting on love.
Shitting on a Tuesday night.
Shitting on shitting.

Bookstore Book vs. Thrift Store Book

While thrift store books smell better,
A crisp, brand new book looks better.

A thrift store book is something
On your list without the personal passion to pull the trigger;
You buy it on a whim
When you see it in the dollar bin.

But then again,
That is what gives it meaning:
"Oh, I have been meaning to read this,
and there it is right there for a buck!"

Thrift store books have the character.
Bookstore books have the class.

A good thrift store book
Is Spook by Mary Roach,
While a good bookstore book
Is a new version of A Tree Grows in Brooklyn.

Buying a book
Is all about giving that book a home.

Music and smells are time machines.

Love is Music/Music is Love

That new song you can't get out of your head...
That old song you sing at the top of your lungs...

A Morrissey shirt says a lot about a person

I think about death
when I clean.

Last week it was the fridge.
This week it's the closet.

The difference is the food
being thrown out is gross.
While the shirts and pants
are mostly fine aside from fit
and a forgotten fondness.

Taking stock of the shelves,
recycling the wire hangers.
Keeping count of the years
and the dangers down the line.

Wondering will I be
the first of the gang to die?
But Kyle beat me to it,
and I toss the mixed greens, of course.

Debating the Morrissey shirt,
for reasons of regret, both ways.

Windex won't wipe away
these doldrums.

Backscratcher

going from Imogen Heap to a 1961 jazz album,
Augusts 10th, between the first coffee at 5am,
and the second coffee at 5:25am, smoking,
and inspiring myself to write: poems before work.

I think it's finally time to accept
that I do not have a mysterious grandmother
who's going to show up and reveal me
as the princess of a small European country.

it's okay, because I love these boring years,
sauntering through my garden, paying bills on time,
watching Jeopardy and skipping the commercials;
I must say, this is living, and I have a backscratcher.

quiet mornings, nothing but music
and the sound of these writing keys,
reading about Doppler frequencies,
because that is what Google gave me.

The little things?
The little moments?
They aren't little.
If I have an itch, I can reach it to scratch it.

Every New Yorker has existed during an impactful moment in music history

From seeing Bob Dylan at Cafe Wha?
to hunting for $.50 50 Cent mix tapes on Canal Street…

From seeing Bon Iver via the Brooklyn folk revival
to listening to Jack Johnson while your daughter
is being born…

From Kings of Leon on Conan
to sneaking into Bowery Ballroom
via the outside smoking section…

Every New Yorker has existed during their own
impactful moment in musical history.

Rock the Dollar Tree

We buy a book for Grandpa Mike
and play badminton inside,
breaking one racket and buying 3,
before leaving to go home with dusty jalapeños.

Mix CD

1. *God Only Knows* by The Beach Boys
2. *Drinking with the Poet* by Scott B. Symphony
3. *Movin' on Up* by Primal Scream
4. *Annie I Wish You'd Quit Drinking* by Fashion Brigade
5. *Jeff's Boogie* by The Yardbirds
6. *Modern Love* by David Bowie
7. *Just Like Honey* by The Jesus and Mary Chain

Playlist

1. *Welcome* by Hey Rosetta!
2. *Bandages* by Hot Hot Heat
3. *Dreamsicle* by Jason Isbell and the 400 Unit
4. *Laugh Track* by Ben Hopkins
5. *Going Gets Tough* by The Growlers
6. *Live Again* by Jane's Party
7. *Ready to Win* by Tokyo Police Club

Sam Evian's Instagram

I am listening to your music
while walking through LaGuardia,
bobbing and weaving between rose tourists,
shucking and jiving through life,
feeling like I am in an early Steven Soderbergh film,
before stealing a book and a bottle
of SmartWater from the Hudson News,
and getting on the plane just in time.

Song

let the borrowed muse rust away
let the cool goddess go
let me live
let my heart become whole again.

Text to Myself: Don't Panic

think about Christmas trees,
and vacay undies,
and people with food stuck in their teeth,
ghosts in general,
grandmas who are about to be ghosts,
and soup that looks so good
but it's way too hot
so you have to wait on it
but then you get impatient
and take a spoonful,
only to burn the roof of your mouth!

If we really get down to brass tacks here

A blood fusion,
like a voodoo ritual,
making the man and his art inseparable,
an unholy bond merging the two into one.

Poem

Played Yeah Yeah Yeahs
while driving with Len today
and now I can hear her singing
Heads Will Roll in her room!

Colorado Roof Repair

One day, we will all be relegated
To a series of snapshots.
So it is important to actually be
In everyday photographs with family;
Not just vacation or destination pictures,
But messy moments and minor memories.

We will try to come to Colorado next year,
But it won't make up for everything.
Even if we were rich and came every month,
You are still only getting vacation time
With the family and the little one,
Which is not as special as the doldrums,
The days in between, the raucous rigmarole,
That is somehow beautiful in passing.

Making compromises is part of life.
Trust me, I don't want to be in Florida,
But that is where the numbers are,
And so far the making of memories
Has been magical here, so I feel bad
That someone special is missing out.

You are right, life is short,
But it is easier for one person (or two)
To make moves than three people
Who have had a helluva couple years,
So keep that in mind, when you beg
To show us the mountains.

Let's Fucking Go

Me, putting the kettle on.
Me, writing and editing poetry on Friday nights.
Me, watching The Food Network.
You, hopefully while reading this.

I wonder what my daughter will save/cherish of mine

Will she wear an old punk shirt
In the halls of her high school?

Will she drink out of the same coffee mugs?

Will she hang my weird art
Along the walls of her home?

Will she read my books, like this one?

Will she collect and display Dad trinkets
And pass them on to her kids,
Turning them into grandfather clocks?

You know what they don't teach ya in school?

That one day you will be
on the bad side of 40,
in a Florida backyard
removing the decaying carcass
of a frog out of the AC grate
when suddenly you pull the head off.

gracias good morning farts

"I respect everything I make fun of."
— John Waters

silly old life.
breach of peace.
myserteous.
hearts and farts.

silent but deadly.
laughing at art.
howling at life.

shell of an engine.
shell of a man.
unlike Humpty Dumpty.
I am putting myself back together.
again.

Under the Service
(Altered Ego)

Here I am,
filling out greeting cards
for babies being born yesterday
and friends of friends
whom I don't really know,
but have their address.

Coyote Blood and Puppy Jones
are under the service of my soul,
but I am just a boy, a simple man,
a baseball fan, a white-knuckled poet
a Jewish father disguised as a tattooed hipster.

Coyote Blood is punk rock
and Puppy Jones is hip-hop,
both are liars, but then again
so are poets, pretty much.

My confidence is only a killer sometimes;
others, it is a wishing well run dry of dreams.
my love is only a lobster dinner at diners;
others, it is leftovers, thrown away one day too late.

There I go,
25 and alive
to 39 and dying
under the service of a forever
so fast I forgot to ask,
what if I am my altered ego,
and those sonsofbitches
are the real me?

Open My Eye Ever So Slightly at 6am

What are we thinking for dinner?
We have those pork chops in the freezer.
Or I could make soup.
I'd never turn down pizza either.

Sad Songs Make Me Happy

the nostalgia of the changing leaves.
the shorter days remind me of newness and fresh air.
love's possibilities and let-downs.

from Bright Eyes to Elliott Smith.
and even one by Taylor Swift ("All Too Well").
sad songs make the season sweeter.

I wish I could turn my brain off forever.
or live in a TV show like One Tree Hill.
or movies that I can recite line for line.

instead of a reprieve from all these feelings.
I wade into them like anti-climactic flood waters.
just drowning in living room longing.

music is the facilitator of feeling forward.
release the regret.
music steps in where language falls short.

it's weird that sounds that someone made.
without you in mind.
can describe something about your own life.
sometimes something that you didn't know affected you.

Friday morning in kitchen.
and I am remembering a time, the time.
who knew emo could have a consoling psychological effect.

I enjoy sad music, but don't enjoy being sad.
I enjoy remembering and being reminded.
of a life lived and loved (and laughed).

solidarity in songs.
says a lot about us in the middle.
a reflection of the/our human condition.

Monday Morning Trader Joe's Music

1. *Breakdown* by Tom Petty
2. *Raspberry Beret* by Prince
3. *All for You* by Sister Hazel
4. *Real Love* by Mary J. Blige
5. *Hey Jealousy* by Gin Blossoms
6. *Easy Money* by Billy Joel
7. *Set Adrift on Memory Bliss* by P.M. Dawn
8. *The King of Wishful Thinking* by Go West

woke up feeling like an artist today!

I am just a blue collar creative,
wearing the same blue jeans all week,
getting all tired (even now) while writing
copy during the day and poetry at night.

Woke up this morning,
not particularly inspired,
but then I was compelled to make things
and an hour in is when it hit.

I don't even notice
when the wave of mutilation tidals
into your heart, down your spine,
and into your spider arms.

Even a solipsistic animal like me
knows nothing matters
because all we are here to do is die,
so why not make things, make money,
and try to smile because...

This poem will live a little longer
than my physical presence,
which just means my kid will get
a little more wiggle room out of my existence.

All artists just want to make things
that will help us live a little longer,
in the middle of the morning
of the big bad universe.

Marquee Moon on Repeat

When I first moved to New York,
I went to CBGB during the day,
and just hung out, wrote, took photos,
inhaled the history.

The door was always open
and no one was ever there;
just me and the famous stage,
just me and the famous toilet.

Besides Bob Dylan,
my soundtrack back then
was Lou Reed,
and Television's Marquee Moon.

I'd imagine what it was like
being in the crowd
when The Ramones tore in
and whipped jowls from howling.

With Tom Verlaine's passing,
a small part of my 20s has died,
but I will always have listening
to Marquee Moon on repeat.

I will always have
that kitchen on 88th street,
and that iPod on the shelf,
when the future was in front of me.

Kites with keys continue to shock us.

Poem (for all the what's and the why's)

I walked to the mailbox,
and read Sylvia's Blue Moles.

At the mailbox,
I received soap,
and got my daughter
a Joe Strummer shirt.

I walked away from the mailbox,
and thanked the sky.

Study Drum

Every minute
Could be the last.

This one.
(A minute later)
Or this one.
(Another sixty seconds of life)

We gather in the flesh
For a new soon,
Never this young again,
But the first time this old.

With a fracture upon my heart,
It exists in two worlds
Yet I am not anxious
Of it ceasing to beat.

I am anxious to forget,
So I learn the moments,
Turn them into forever
And find a way to remember.

Every moment
Could be the first.

Brown Thumbs Up Emoji

Been leaving my phone
at home
on weekends.

Going out
and getting lost,
living life
with my eyes.

No matter the city,
no matter the secrets,
all I want is a little home
near enough to a creek
I can hear it.

That's where,
one day,
I will throw my phone
forever.

Ode to My First Gray Pube

While it does have its fringe benefits—
eating cookies whenever I want, sex,
grocery shopping takes on a zen-like exorcise—
getting old does, indeed, suck.

I had to do a double take.
It was July 4th, 2022.
I was drying off after a shower,
and I looked down, thinking *hmmm…*
"What the hell is that?" I said aloud.

There was no question:
Growing on my bushy balls
was a white—not blonde—hair.
I am 39 at the time of writing this.

Finding your first grey hair is an uncanny experience
no matter where it is.
My mustache held my very first grey hair,
somewhere around the age of 30.

Choosing to go full bush
marks me as a man
exhorted by neither giving a shit
or wanting to waste the time.

Aging isn't something
that happens to your old face,
or just your grandmother
on your mother's side.

I forgot
crotches are not

supposed to be
fountains of youth, too.

I wonder if Michael Jordan's pubes are still black,
despite him going bald at a young age;
I wonder if Brad Pitt shaves
his doubtlessly gray pubes.

It's silly that one hair
down their
can make me feel closer to death,
but it does and I don't like it.

I tweezer it out,
because I guess I am a self-ageist.

Steamboat and a Brooklyn 99 GIF

I have Berlin's song
The Metro
Stuck in my head,
As I sit cross-legged
On the 2 train,
Going uptown for brekkie
At Tom's Restaurant.

Stabbed & Been Stabbed

You can be selfish and selfless.

One time outside a bar in Harlem
I guessed a man's age and weight
And he gave me his Yankee's hat
Right off his head.

I wish I still had that hat.

I wonder if I was right
Or if this was
A Nate Bargatze
John/Jane Doe situation?

It certainly changed me

your writing might not change the world
but it will change you and that's enough.

Policeman's Heel

A dead frog hangs in the air conditioner,
I can do nothing about it.

My heel hurts
And I feel like I am walking on glass bones,
I can do nothing about it.

Time keeps ticking away,
Never to return,
I can do nothing about it.

My daughter starts third grade tomorrow,
I can do nothing about it.

Her hands are still tiny,
I can do nothing about it.

I'll be up early,
Listening to music,
Drinking coffee,
Hammering the typer keys,
I can do nothing about it.

Holy. Hell.

Heaven is
Mornings,
Chocolate chip French toast,
Bacon,
And Devendra Banhart,
Her.

Hammer Theory

Aspire is your ritual,
your intention,
and deliberate daily actions.

It's the space between you
and your achievements.

Emotional states of the opposite valence occur
following the ending of an initial emotional state.
Thus the ending of one emotion (e.g., happiness)
automatically brings on the start of the opposite emotion
(e.g., sadness),
and vice versa, Plato.

How strange would appear to be this thing
that humans call pleasure!
And how curiously it is related to what is thought to be
its opposite, pain!

Acquired motives, like love,
sensory cravings and thrill-seeking behavior,
as well as needs for power,
achievement and affiliation,
operate by obeying empirical laws.

Abraham Maslow wrote in 1966,
"If the only tool you have is a hammer,
it is tempting to treat everything as if it were a nail."

Life goes up
and life goes down
and life goes round and round.
Whack!

You don't have to read a book to love it.

I still haven't read The Goldfinch,
But when I see it on the shelf
Of a hipster hotel it hits my heart hard.

And I never finished The Midnight Library,
Because it was too hard at the time,
But I own like six copies.

These books bring me
Above ground for a second,
Just from sight of cover,
Smell of page.

I bought a book in Wyoming once—
Letters of a Pioneer Woman—
Never read it,
But when I see its spine on my bookshelf
A mini movie plays in my brain.

Perfect Night

After writing.
I preheat the oven.
Jerk off.
Put the cookies in.
Read a book.
Take the cookies out.
Put on music while the cookies cool.
Fold laundry.
Eat cookies in bed.
While falling asleep to Seinfeld.

I don't break the rules until I know I can

what if we are in the matrix, but it is also a physical world?
like we are actual roaming, skin-covered, robot avatars,
but thoughts, feelings, etc are just a computer program!

Doldrums, grace and mud...

amendatory muon

All stress is cumulative;
the sky's far dome is sane and clear.

There is a promenade
with pretty people
sipping merlot and making small talk,
wasting their wonderful lives
exactly how they desire,
where midnights are enough
to wash the tears away.

There is a version of me
sitting on that same patio,
not thinking of love and death,
or transfiguration of the soul;
there is a simpler pseudo Ryan,
that is unencumbered by inspiration,
petrichor, the past or the future.

I like who I am,
but I often wonder
what it would be like
to just be thrilled by a steady paycheck,
a police procedural,
weekend cornhole with friends from work,
and other low-level excitabilities.

There is another type of person
who lives in a Plath poem,
full of wondering at dead moles,
without the ego fighting the id,
days are days and that is enough.

In the middle of the pass is a brattice
in which a man always stands guard,
shouting loudly, "Enemy!" at anyone
who passes him by and happens to lock eyes,
and I can't help but wonder
what his stresses added up to bring him here.

All stress is cumulative;
the sky's far dome is sane and clear.

Adulting Hard Today

From the devil dentist
to a heavenly haircut,
a good-spirited hygienist
to a gangster Puerto Rican,
end on the hellacious DMV.

No stranger to the beauty and sadness of juxtaposition
but a twist is in store that's sure to encourage:
There is no such thing as adulting:
There is no such thing as growing up:
Biological age cannot be an indicator:
A source of income cannot be a dictator.

The laughter that disguises you as a sufferer
is apt for Twitter and synonymous with Wordpress.

You can be almost 40 but still behave like a toddler,
because age, intellect, experience
and memory don't matter:
Clarity of thought, clarity in action
is what everyone wants, just pay attention.

Stages of life are only byproducts of imagination,
and my maturity turns out to be a mischievous crocodile,
thus you still need to grin with sharpened sins.

No one told us
that life would just be
a series of running
errands.

Poem

my role has changed,
I am not the same,
and I cannot abide
by the past any longer.

my role has changed,
I am not the same,
and I either lay weak
or grow stronger.

my role has changed,
I am not the same,
maybe more muscle
maybe less sinew.

my role has changed,
I am not the same,
reassuring my daughter,
I tell her "the future is in you."

The Sum of This Loud House

The house is quiet
except for the shower water,
draining through the pipes in the walls,
going down past me in the dining room
and off into the underground of I don't know.

My daughter is singing up there,
this is the nicest dwelling
I have ever lived in
(I used to think people with stairs were rich),
and I hope she knows how lucky she is.

I sure am lucky,
looking around at the big kitchen
which is stocked with snacks,
plants on the windowsill,
expensive laptop just for shitty poems.

The house is quiet,
except for the ice being made in the freezer,
clunking down into the bin,
which is half frozen all the time,
just an idiosyncratic quirk
of a loud love-filled house.

Taking stock real quick,
I have everything I need,
from 100+ t-shirts to health
and a happy kid
and I will always be right here,
amazed that I am alright.

Kismet of the Clock

I write down ideas for money.
(poems for hope)
This autumn, my dreams become jealous.
(of that which I actually achieve)

My favorite color is October.
(but it's still September)
My favorite heart is hers.
(but I'll never break it again)

I bet you're infinite.
(This is the matrix)
I wait for the train.
(I know what forever feels like)

Time has a good sense.
(of humor)
I set a reminder.
(to feel my chemical imbalance)

When people ask what I do.
(I tell them I put commas in the wrong place)
They don't get it or me.
(but fate does)

Oy Vey

I wonder if Basquiat cared about how he smelled.
I wonder what Sylvia Plath would think of the Food Network.
I wonder if Ocean Vuong shops at Old Navy.
I wonder what Rimbaud would think of me.

Old Sun, Young Moon

I took
a rare Friday night off
from writing
last week.

I tried
but laziness
and lethargy
got the best of me.

I suffer,
you suffer,
we all suffer,
but comparative suffering ain't good for nobody.

I don't
depend on you,
but I had nothing tonight
about which to write.

I am an iceberg,
I am unctuous,
I am a head of let us,
I am toxic shock syndrome.

I welcome
the death of my youth
like a professional athlete
welcomes their retirement from sport.

Umm, Thanks!

Yesterday, the dental hygienist
Told me the same bacteria found in unchecked teeth
Is the same bacteria that causes Alzheimer's
And that the cells under a microscope
Look like spiders with legs and all,
And that is something I will now never forget,
And now I am gonna end this poem and go floss.

Never Medium Rare

Maybe home isn't a place
but a series of moments
in which you feel less alone.

    - From "Antares" by Damian Rucci

I, myself, have never cooked a steak properly.
Grill or pan upon stovetop,
I always overcook them.

Best steak I ever had
was not at a fancy place in Downtown Manhattan,
but a Chili's by the Orlando International Airport.

I burned the steak tonight,
a rib-eye from Trader Joe's
that I marinated overnight in Brazilian butcher salt.
I undercooked the jalapeño poppers.
The steak is too salty,
so I chop it up and save it to accompany tomorrow's eggs,
and eat a stale apple cider doughnut,
also from Trader Joe's.

After dinner, I empty the coffee machine,
spilled grounds in the impossible-to-clean crevices
of the garbage can kick-lid.
I take out the garbage.

It's raining but I never believed in umbrellas,
so I get a poetic sprinkle upon my face and shoulders,
as the petrichor seeps into my soul
and I stand there for a little bit longer,
just feeling the falling night sky water,

before going back inside, where it smells like burnt meat
(and probably will all weekend),
and watch the Yankees game while reading a book.

The Yankees are honoring Derek Jeter tonight
with a plaque in Monument Park.
I miss New York City.

My daughter sings a song upstairs,
a song that seems made-up and probably is;
I stop missing New York City.

I get distracted by my phone,
and inevitably Instagram, then Twitter,
but I am pulled back to Earth,
when Aaron Hicks makes an error,
and my daughter starts singing again.

Poem

I can rest my eyes for an hour
or I can risk my life for a day,
no matter the knife or stress,
everything is going to be okay.

To the Sucker Punch of My Childhood Files

I didn't know how bad it was until I got out
And made friends with other kids
Who thought they had it bad
And then we shared stories and they were like
"Oh shit, well at least I don't have it that bad,"
They'd say and then we would watch MTV
And then go off into the woods to look for porno mags.

Why were there always porno mags
hidden in the woods in the 90s?
Why were we always in the woods?
Making bike jumps and forts until porno was found
In a bag under a log just off a path
Between wet ferns and so many tires.

I thought Heavy Metal and Rap was all there was,
Because every older brother liked Heavy Metal,
And every older sister liked Rap,
And that's all there was, siblings and the radio,
No moms or dads, at least in my case.

Some days, especially in the summer,
There would be fights between friends,
And some days during the school year,
There would be fights
between rollerbladers and skateboarders,
But nothing more than bloodied egos and swollen eyes,
Mostly from crying because the adrenalin catapulted
Our emotions like a trebuchet out our faces
And we did not know what to do, except run home, lie,
Saying we fell out of a tree when a tree snail bit us,
And then hide until the house went to the bar
While listening to Cypress Hill's Black Sunday CD
on a school night.

Swallowing Panic in the Face of the Sword

Comprehending the end.
Thinking about the back of my knee.
Listening to Joanna Newsom.
And still feeling confident about it all.

I stand by my opinion.
Separate should be.
Spelled with an E after the P.
like Seperate.

From a cosmic perspective.
Laughter is the best foreplay,
But from the bedroom.
That is not the case.

Even spider-filled seashells exist.
Think about it.
Probably in Louisiana.
Odds are weirder.

How Long Do You Think It's Gonna Last?

Ranedon

I don't want to be a mad dad;
I want to be a glad dad.

The day is filled
With lots of emotions—
From morning caffeinated confidence
To wit's end weekday evenings
After a long day of work.

Despite patience—
Or lack thereof—
I am trying to get a handle
On the waves,
The ups and down.

She is my buoy,
My boogie board, too,
And I always want
To be fun and happy
For my little Charlie Bucket.

Playing Baseball with Walt Whitman

Being self-aware is crazy.

But it will steal our bases
and be a burden to us.

Chiefest of all is love.

But it will repair our losses
and be a blessing to us.

B.I.C.O.E: Books In Case Of Emergency

I keep two books on the coffee table:
Call Us What We Carry, poems by Amanda Gorman,
and *You Are Here* by Thich Nhat Hanh.

I leave them there as break-in-case-of-emergency books,
easily bringing one with me to places in which
I know I am in for a long wait.

I also like that my daughter sees them every day,
and that she sees me reading other books on the couch;
today's was *Widow Basquiat*,
and yesterday's was *The Man Who Invented Motion Pictures*.

She is in third grade and learning to read;
I sure hope she falls in love with words
way before I did in life,
because I was 18 and stubborn,
which turned me into a book snob for years.

The books on the coffee table
have ketchup splatters from different dinners,
coffee spots from many mornings;
they are part of our lives
and they matter.

Even if they don't move or get read
until a long overdue doctor visit
means filling out forms and waiting
and reading.

All doctors' offices should have a breakfast buffet
and a library,
but until they do,

I will always grab a book
before heading out the door.

And hopefully these books play a subconscious,
subliminal role in my child's choices,
for wealth or health.

God

There is something so gorgeous
About eating latkes and sour pickles
In a Queens diner at midnight
After a standup comedy show.

We Live in Ron Perlman's Matrix

We were hungry
and stuck in Greenpoint,
because of my feet
being made of broken glass,
so we went to eat at Paulie Gee's,
which is gangster pizza,
and I highly recommend the Hellboy®.

Behind the bar,
I noticed a lone VHS tape cover
propped up on display,
so I asked the ageless hipster bartender,
and she proudly announced
that it was Hellboy,
starring Ron Perlman.

I proceed to tell
anyone who will listen
about seeing that film by myself
in Downtown Orlando, Florida,
right after ending things
my with college girlfriend,
whose name was/is Stephanie with a PH.

The bartender proceeds to tell
anyone that will listen
that if Ron Perlman were to ever come in there
she would "buy his dinner and take his ugly ass home,"
which resulted in more laughs
than my Stephanie story.

Later that evening,
we drank club sodas

and smoked disposable weed pens,
on the roof of a cool hotel bar with a pool,
in which no one was permitted to swim,
and then we witnessed a fight
in an entrance line.

But then my tired, inebriated mind was blown,
when I laid eyes upon
the one-and-only Ron Perlman
walking into the hotel as we were walking out,
and all I could do was scream his name,
because what are the freaking odds?

What is your concern, Ray?

The one moment.
The soldier's moment.
The lover's moment.
In either battle, that's all you get.
One moment of everything at once.
And anything before is nothing.
Everything after...nothing.
Nothing in comparison...to that one moment.

Didn't you get enough moments?

Seems not, doesn't it?

what happens when we die?

it's only conjecture
but I imagine it will be exactly the same before I was here,
which makes it incumbent upon us
to create a literal heaven on earth,
never a hell.

coyote hills

we lived for a while
in a house in the hills.

the coyotes would start
their song at dawn.

dawn and dusk
were their main appearance times.

the coyotes would come take notes,
edging closer every day.

mornings were my king,
like a righteous floating tide.

the coyotes would drift
into our world.

predator and prey blurred,
the past and the present blurred.

the reality is
I was their future.

I've pointed out many a pretty sky,
and it's either kids or coyotes.

Real life only happens on yesterdays' couches

They are upstairs,
practicing their lines;
the play doesn't open
until February, but…

I read downstairs,
while the Yankees game is on;
before bed I have to do the dishes,
and tomorrow is garbage day.

I remember I have to steal
packets of Splenda from the bodega,
and tell my sister what I want for my bday;
maybe I should say a Costco box of Splenda?

Water the raspberries out back, too,
clean Goldie and call Veronica,
watch Nathan For You,
and sweep the back patio.

Poem

Repetition breeds confidence.
But it also creates craziness.

Wet Wednesdays

dreams come true
even on wet Wednesdays.

the dirt on the back
of this Orlando Magic hat
is from Bukowski's grave.

our shoes and hats
have traveled with us
from ocean to ocean.

what a strange vine,
summoned for unceremoniousness.

inanimate objects,
like necklaces,
hang in the balance of our being.

in the key of meaning,
you either find your color
or it slips right by ya.

because moments do, too,
and early aspirations.
couples who fart together, stay together.

now discuss.

seriously,
stop reading this "poem"
and go fart and talk about it
with your loved ones.

Pansnakes for the Table

you could tell me I am dying
and I think I would handle it better
than if my computer stopped working,
especially if I was in the middle of a Gmail draft.

once a denizen of the cauldron,
aware of the times through which we are passing,
but still my ego and residual adolescence
combine to get the best of me in biting moments,
however trivial or just dumb they may be.

a lover who listens,
a local "run errands with me" friend,
because, no, I don't want to spend $85 on dinner,
but I will go to Costco and a yard sale with you,
and then get some pancakes and gossip.

my emotion cadence is that of a motorcycle dying—
the day is filled with a lot of vrooms and chokes,
but we are all doing our best
and at least, yikes, I am hyper-self-aware.

This poem is too good for a title

Just took the little one
to the park across the street
cuz a bunch of her friends
had a flag football game.

I am grateful for how all the other kids
freaked when they saw her,
waving from the field,
running up and giving her hugs.

To give my daughter a "normal" childhood,
however suburban, is invaluable to me,
but to watch her life unfold is wild,
and to watch her feel special is wonderful.

She looked so happy
and that is all that matters,
and that is why
I do not drink anymore.

Forever, I hope.

praying hands emoji
for impending Q4.

queue the Imperial March music,
because in the e-commerce world,
shit is about to get dark.

list maker and note taker,
a blue collar creative ready to write,
sometimes ya gotta slam
that delete key.

writing this
on a brand new
MacBook Pro,
wish I were more excited,
but embracing who I am,
truth to power.

most things are bullshit,
only a couple things are life.

one day you will have your last bite of pizza.
Sausage, pepperoni...think about that for a second.

I am at the intersection of music and comedy,
with a back up degree in dirt merchant poetry.

I hope my last bite of pizza is something good,
from a no-name place in NYC (not Papa John's).

No More NFT Talk

we are putting that behind us.
the real world is king once again.
do drugs and go to a museum.

What if the Devil doesn't know he is the Devil?

"Life has become immeasurably better since
I have been forced to stop taking it seriously."
- Hunter S. Thompson

I hope one day
someone makes a documentary
about me.

It would make
for a fun Sunday watch
for art nerds
who are distracted
on their future phones.

I'd like to believe
I have a good story,
rags to...regular.

There is something to be said
about a stubborn poet,
who mails editors postcards
made of recycled VHS covers.

Everyday, I shake my fist
at God for giving me
good taste with no inherited wealth.

Better than the opposite though, right?
It's like I am a character in a Jane Austen novel.

I lived fast,
but I didn't die young,

so now what?

My message will be
it is okay and allowed
to be both happy and sad.

Maybe I'm too much,
and maybe I'm never enough;
maybe that's how I will be.

Judge

The record is 61
Hit in 1961,
Which was 61 years ago.

Not All Lies Are Untrue

I exist in multiple worlds...

somewhere between a kid wanting to be Indiana Jones
and a grown man wanting to live
with more than just a laugh.

add a splash of poetry and a dash of stubbornness,
and you got yourself a Ryan Buynak cocktail
that is not for everybody, especially the faint of heart,
even though I am faint of heart myself.

that Disney-loving kid is still in there somewhere,
underneath the wannabe beard, the hipster skin,
and the fear of missing out on death itself,
hoping that in the place prior to rain,
among the petrichor and past lives,
is love that never gives up, even when she gives up.

a young gangster versus an aging pugilist,
it is something out of something that crosses a movie,
a dramedy that deserves an Oscar for lies and time,
this the space surrounding a hiding place,
but I am "It" in this game, seeking something
that resembles peace in the living room
but confidence in the corner.

a little bit hip hop and a little bit punk rock,
balancing being both Beetlejuice
and an Adam Sandler character,
realizing too late my sexual awakening came
during the first watch of the music video
for Natalie Imbruglia's *Torn*,
and to this day I would rather a unique hipster girl in jeans

with sad blue eyes than a cliche hot blonde in yoga pants.

I contain multitudes despite being basic sometimes, too,
and just buying a Bob Dylan shirt on sale at Kohl's,
then eating a chimichanga with my daughter,
during which she asks me about death and I have to lie,
and say that it will be a long time before I die,
that someday is such a distant tomorrow
and it's just like falling asleep.

NAIP
(not another internet profile!)

11:08am:
HR woman
with too many Ys in her name
Slacks me,
asking me to leave a review
for the company,
which means...
yep...
you guessed it...
setting up another
goddamn internet profile!

Devils:
I do not want to do this,
so I put it off,
hoping she would forget,
when another employee asks
if I have had to do this,
and I tell her yes,
but I don't want to,
because, yep...
you guessed it...
another goddamn internet profile!

A week later:
I still have yet to do it,
but now
I am hoping
that I am the one to forget,
because I simultaneously
feel guilty, but
don't want to do it,

because, yep...
you guessed it...
another goddamn internet profile!

Caffeinated & Celebrated

Random Thursday Thoughts...

There is a sweet spot in the morning—
after the coffee has kicked in,
but before the day has kicked my ass—
where I feel like I can conquer
a medium-sized city like Cleveland
with confidence and creativity.

I have to go to a wedding today,
but honestly, who schedules a wedding
on a Thursday afternoon,
on Groundhog Day, no less?!?

My hot take is that most of us
have not adequately processed the trauma of the pandemic,
and our sprawling, unprocessed trauma
chews away at our brains
in myriad ways that make us anxious about why
we can't seem to live our lives as instinctively
as we did in 2019.

I don't drink anymore
so I don't write about the moon anymore,
or maybe it is vice versa:
me versus the universe
or the universe versus me?

This is how old I am:
I put a note in my phone
to remind myself
to cut my toe nails later.

From plot point to plot point,
my raison d'etre isn't just about survival,
it's about *what* is keeping us alive,
and what we're keeping alive:
will the last of moments know things like love?

Young Ryan would simply be stoked
to know that I now have two t-shirts
from two different record stores in LA.

Throwback Syndrome

Nostalgia is eating up the airwaves,
and the retail rotundas;
everything is 90s this and 90s that,
everything 90s is back.

Just as when I was a kid,
and everything was 70s,
but we are further from the 90s now,
than we were the 70s then.

The phone feeds into my childhood urge
to just keep scrolling through cable channels,
but now it is Instagram Reels
of people falling, music and basketball.

But why did the worst fashion of the era return—
the clunky Filas and Reeboks,
minus the baby-doll crop-tops and the JNCOs—
and not much for men but a continuation of flannel shirts.

Instead of GoodFellas and Seinfeld,
I will watch something new tonight,
but then I see Empire Records on Hulu,
and I nod like Lady Gaga in the meme.

Can't help but to have
a "kids these days" kind of vibe,
but I am soooo glad I was young and crazy
before there were cell phones and evidence.

Have a knife life!

333: half the evil

I am proof
Being a better person
Is possible.

Now, I am not
A completely new,
Altruistic human.

I am just
Slightly better
At living.

I know how to Friday night!

Listening to a Miles Davis record
and reading Rolling Stone magazine;
I know how to Friday night!

All those "old" people
who used to come in
to Alice's Tea Cup...
I'm their age now.

I found a receipt
from that time,
from the post office
on the Upper East Side.

Scratching my beard,
I craft this poem
in the kitchen,
without a fresh batch
of bullshit to inspire.

Just 3 jobs,
plus literature—
which isn't a job,
but a lifestyle
(or just a life,
but not just)—
and 3 calls,
plus gorgeous.

On the back of the receipt,
there is a note that just says
"The Yankees beat the Mariners,"
not a complete unknown.

In the light,
I can see a series
of indentions on the paper,
as if I wrote on another
piece of paper
on top of this one.

This says
"I commute downtown,
juicin' it."

It's been years since
I woke up
and just laid in bed.
Maybe tomorrow I will try this.

It's the new one
with boygenius on the cover;
I know how to Friday night!

**when it's my time to call your bluff
I'll call you beautiful and leave it alone**

What is the most devastating line
from a musical of all time
and why is it
"I think there's a time
to come to New York
and a time to leave."?

I went from a Central Florida mallrat
to a South Florida Target possum,
with a lifetime in between,
and those are the years
I am most famous for.

Counting on you alone
to rip your guts out,
I am not Isaac Bashevis
so I can't sing to you in Yiddish
how to live your life,
but I will find my freedom
and help you find yours.

Welcome to Smokescreen Season

It's another heavy day
in a heavy world…

Our strategy of ignoring real problems
and fighting fake ones does not seem to be working.

Let me be extremely clear,
this decision is not about
pro-life vs pro-choice
or religious vs non-religious.

This is about dividing and conquering.
They want us to fight and divide
so they can conquer.

It'd be easy to fix America
but you'd have to piss off
a lot of stupid people
who think this is black and white.

Scheduling a group hug
in Parkland tomorrow at 4:00 pm.
We need it.

There is no drug as good as confidence

Writing is a byproduct
Of the hunt and the haunt.

Hunting a better life,
Bigger love,
A better understanding
Of the bigger universe
And your place in it.

That which haunts you
As you go along your journey;
The trials and tribulations,
The fails and the fun,
All of it under the sun,
And over the moon.

The opposite of never
is just a Tuesday in June.
Allen Ginsberg's dad
Was a poet,
And I hope I can be
Half as half as him.

One day we will be
Remembered.
My doctor told me today
That I am gonna live
To one-hundred-years-old.

here goes everything

this morning I sent my novel manuscript
to a literary agent for consideration,
and laid it all—ego, heart, future—on the table
for her to eat with hamburger or help with hustle.

a simple email, I wonder if Iris knows
how goddamn hard it was for me
to hit 'Send' and let it go out into the universe;
I hope she does, because I believe
that in the right hands this thing could be magical.

I wrote the first line in 2009,
and believed from that moment
that this will be a collection of wild words
for which I will spurn my soul.

all we can do in this life is try,
and this morning I tried with all my might,
putting a piece of myself
out into the wild blue yonder
to be judged and fated, for good or ill.

this is not the end,
but a new chapter (pun intended),
and whatever happens
it is just a small step in my spiral staircase timeline.

Unbridled Enthusiasm

good music.
good work.
good morning.

clear eyes.
full heart.
can't lose.

did you just quote Friday Night Lights
in a poem, she asked.
You bet your ass I did,
I said.

Life is good.
I am afraid.

So I make jokes,
and dated pop culture references.

Drink my coffee too fast,
wish for San Francisco,
cuz these pretzels
are making me thirsty.

Poem

sometimes the blues is a passing bird
and sometimes it is a stone thrown upon my shoulder
either way it is something to be held fast
because even the blues barely last.

Transfigurations

do wild horses still exist?

this is Jim Harrison's November.
the hammer lost,
but returning like
the soul of dogs.

while I simultaneously
fry up some pork belly,
watch poetry, write poetry,
other lives play in pots and pans,
penning poetry but probably
passing away.

per percentage,
more people die
than really live.
Pete Hill is just gone,
Kyle is ten years gone.

when you see death
so much as a child,
it numbs you to it
for a big chunk of your life.

your teachers are dying,
and I am as proud of the poetry
as I am the pork belly.

my fear of death is back,
but that means life is worth living again.

wild horses still exist.

have an unstoppable day

watching Peaky Blinders
and supplementing it
with a lighter show like
Reboot on Hulu.

the latter of which
won't last,
but then again,
nothing lasts.

good nights give way
to unstoppable days,
and I believe in the power
of positive thinking this morning.

with a smile on my face,
wind in my hair,
coffee in my veins,
I woke up to play and create.

Poem

I don't write poems to tell important stories;
I write poems to make sad hipsters kiss.
I saw the best writers of my generation
become 'content strategists.'

Journal Square and Jungian therapy

Wisecracks are existential rescues
of imperiled self-possession,
worth the risk of a punch to the gut,
and conserving calm the noticing world.

I listen to Bon Iver on the morning of my 40th birthday
and think about the kid in his twenties,
listening to Bon Iver in Union Square,
writing in his journal and falling in love.

All I have ever done is make wisecracks about life and love,
while trying to remember to write them down
during visceral, life-changing moments.

Advice to aspiring youth:
in New York, the years that you spend as a nobody
are painful but golden, because no one bothers
to lie to you.

October 26th is the day Marty McFly goes back in time,
and my borrowed muse being, I guess, the grim reaper.

I've often quoted Baudelaire:
"I cultivated my hysteria with terror and delight."
But I also thrilled to the august sanities
of "systematic derangement of the senses" (Rimbaud).

I can see the paragraphs I'm writing as little Hells,
penning me into perspectives, conceits, ideas, jokes,
and memories—stories!
Not an original type of anxiety, for a writer.

I am more of an anthropologist these days,

with personal and coterie loyalties,
moments of feeling special,
before feeling as meaningless as minutes vs moments.

Can I pause, slow down life?
I always said that when my time comes
I'd want to go fast,
but where's the fun in that?

Between bulletins from my body that say this isn't so,
I still feel like a kid inside,
writing wisecracks on the outside
to save my ego and soul.

Endeavoring to practice self-forgiveness,
poetry affords me a bonus credit
for hopefully increasing human happiness.
But a devil in me exulted.

Reality is always droning on as usual,
with impartial sunlight streaming through a nearby
window and picking up swirls of dust motes,
I emerge, a tattered scarecrow.

We may be accidents of matter and energy,
but we can't help circling back to the sense of a meaning
that is unaccountable by the application of what we know.

I've had big romances, small loves,
sure,
and have the rest of my life be a tragicomedy.

everyyearfields

in honor of the new year,
I will try again to recite
Gregory Corso's "Marriage,"
as I do every year,
to the chagrin of my friends,
sans champagne now, of course,

but one must earn
that velvet hood somewhere,
along with black heart emojis,

Falstaffian poetry
in the last halcyon days,
saving praise for later,

conflicted fuckers remain
inexplicably silent,
despite New Year's Eve
being just another night.

should I be good?

resist change
at your own peril,
they say.

Reluctant Floridian

Despite what anyone tells you,
This place is hot, expensive, and the only culture
In the middle of the shopping center maze,
Is another shopping centre spelled differently.

Summer is 11 months long,
And we hardly ever go to the beach,
But it is best for the kid,
And I have to accept that.

But I don't have to like it,
And I don't have to love the bugs, the driving, the people,
Or the fact that one good bagel place
is a little too far, a little too much.

My only hope is that
When the kid goes to college,
She goes somewhere north
And we can follow.

The Invaluableness of Solidarity

Judge me against the commoner, not the king.

Humor is like one of my tertiary aesthetics…

I choose not to call upon it,
but it's always lingering there,
like death,
over all this other stuff.

The Depth of Darkness, The Importance of Nothing, Nostalgia and the Future

I descend the stairs not knowing
that my sister, who had just flown back to Colorado,
had sent me 45 photographs of our wayward family—
my Grandfather (who died when I was 2 months old
and whom I look like more and more as I age),
my mom and her first husband (said sister's father),
aunts and uncles, smoking on farm-looking front porches.

How do I show and relate these images to my daughter?
How do I tell her about all the lives we live?
I was once a boy in the backyard.
I was once a skinny teenager, chasing tennis balls and girls.
I was never good at sitting still.

I was listening to this interview just the other day
with Rick Rubin
and he was talking about working with AC/DC.
Rubin was saying how when he was producing them,
they'd just sit around all day in the studio drinking coffee
and smoking cigarettes.

Rubin would get antsy, point to his watch,
and the lead guitarist, Angus Young—
who was really the heart and soul of the band—
would just point to the cigarette in his hand like...
What the fuck do you want me to do? I'm smoking.
I can't play guitar while I'm smoking.

What Rubin later realized was that AC/DC's genius
didn't just come from them "doing"
but from them "doing nothing."

The band knew they only had 3-4 creative sprints
in them a day, and so like a pride of lions,
they'd lie around for hours at a time,
shooting the shit until inspiration struck.
Then, they'd put down their cigarettes,
pick up their instruments and hunt.

I wonder if humanity isn't worse off
spending 12 hours a day staring owl-eyed at their screens,
instead of doing nothing and just waiting for inspiration.

My aunt and uncle visiting
from their Illinois country home
taught me how to be okay with sitting still,
a quality that has been as important
to my career as anything.

To be a decent writer (and father),
you have to be okay with
either doing everything or doing absolutely nothing.

I'm a firm believer that a great way to be creative
is to sit around and do nothing
until you get bored enough to entertain yourself.

Yesterday, for example, the words weren't coming.
So, I spent hours sitting around, sipping coffee,
watching *Wednesday* on Netflix,
painting, and not writing jack shit.
I wish I would have had a pack of cigarettes,
maybe I would have felt better about doing nothing.
But, really, I did absolutely nothing of importance,
nothing of productivity.

That's writing, though.
Some days you do nothing.

Other days, you do something.
But, the only way to have the days where you do something
is to be okay with the days where you doing nothing,

And then some days you get scared of the dark,
sacred of the past, so terrified of the future...
that you sit and write the present
like a goddamn thunderstorm locomotive
barreling down the track of your chest, out of your heart,
raising hell into the wild new now.

Today, I am volunteering at my daughter's school's bookfair,
and I will get a lot of invaluable living
from these moments which had such an impact
on me as a kid (even though I could not afford
a bookmark Lamborghini poster),
so it is cool to know that I will be in the memories
when my child is old and nostalgic
like I apparently am at this moment.

Oppugn

To be a skateboarder,
you have to be okay with pain,
the pain of falling off the skateboard.

You have to be okay with the skinned knees,
bruised elbows, broken tailbones and concussions.

This willingness to accept pain
is what separates the skateboarder from the wannabe
just like it separates the professional from the amateur
in any vocation.

There are a lot of people in this world
that like the idea of being something until they are faced
with the painful costs of becoming that something.

While I get the sentiment,
Charles Bukowski's line about finding something you love
and letting it kill you is a bit dramatic
and, perhaps, toxic in creating a well-balanced life.

However, I do think all of us
should find something we love
and let it hurt us.

"Does this parcel contain anything fragile, liquid, perishable, or potentially hazardous, including lithium batteries and perfume?"

If virtuosity is all that a poet can display,
if his poems demand attention
simply because of their elaborateness and difficulty,
then he has in some sense failed.

I am…in love (not wisely but too well) with language itself.
Too often the result is tedious foolery,
the language run amok with Jabberwocky possibility
(words, words, monotonously inbreeding),
as if possibility were reason enough for the doing.

Everyone interested in contemporary poetry
should read random books hidden on dusty shelves…
In our time of tired mirrors
and more-than-tiresome confession,
the prize is the rare poet who writes
through the looking glass.

Dad Sneezes

My sneezes are getting louder,
I've noticed.

Not as loud
as Ran Balagan.

But nearing
Dad level loudness.

It is only
a matter of time.

Until my sneezes
disrupt a service.

Teens in the Street

I forgot something in my truck
so I opened the loud garage,
and outside beyond the truck
a group of teen boys
were hanging in the street.

I open the truck
via the keychain remote
and grab sunglasses
from the glovebox.

I look up and realize
the boys are gone,
scattered into the night,
and that's when I realize…

To them I am the man,
the old neighbor man,
and my existence flashes,
and I feel fragile.

I am jealous of those boys
with their whole life
in front of their eyes
and nothing can stop them!

They are the stars
of their own movie,
and everything is an adventure,
and this is just the beginning of their films.

I am the old man,
the old neighbor man with the truck,

and tattoos and the beard,
and I am already in the middle of my movie.

Get your H out of your A

Your art
will follow
your heart.

**Anytime she wants to play basketball.
I play every time.**

Pull out the hoop
I scored from the free section
of the Nextdoor App
at the very beginning of the panda.

Gotta remember,
she only wants to play for a little,
and she will only ask me to play
for a couple more years.

No matter if I am working,
waiting, eating, or dying…
if she asks,
I will play.

The ball needs air,
but the evening air is nice,
and I, the luckiest dude alive,
get to shoot hoops with my daughter.

Anytime she wants to play Legends of the Hidden Temple. I play every time.

Pull off all the covers,
throw most of the pillows on the floor,
except for the one we use
for obstacles and inside jokes.

Gotta remember,
she only wants to play for a little,
and she will only ask me to play
for a couple more years.

No matter if I am working,
waiting, eating, or dying…
if she asks,
I will play.

The games are silly and simple,
but the smiles are nice and real,
and I, the luckiest dad alive,
get to stoke my child's imagination.

Response Poem

There is nothing more hipster
Than reading a Pitchfork article
About the albums Chloe Sevigny loves
At a tattoo shop
Where I am about to get
The cover of my second book of poetry
Tattooed on my left bicep
Just above the pencil tattoo of the NYC skyline.

But instead of being in Brooklyn,
I am in Deerfield Beach, Florida,
And I am old, turning 40,
And this is my gift to myself,
Because the book came out ten years ago, too,
Or more, I don't know,
Because it has been so long.

Last night I ate
A sneaky donut
In the kitchen,
Not expecting to be inspired,
But I was because
Of how far I have come:
From the Central Florida white ghettos
To coming of age in Manhattan
And on to the lessons I learned,
All of it response
That led me here
To happiness and hindsight.

And apparently,
You can take the hipster out of Brooklyn,
But you can't take the hipster out of me.

**True confidence is
moving forward in uncertainty**

Just Once

I want abs
just once
and I want to post
a photo of myself
shirtless on Instagram
with awesome abs
just once.

Hope is as Hard as Hammers

People speak of Hope
as if it is this delicate, ephemeral thing
made of whispers and cobwebs.

It's not.

Hope has dirt on its face,
blood on its knuckles
the grit of a tooth just spat out
onto the cobblestones,
only to rise for another go.

2023 New Year's Resolutions

1. Shop the novel
2. Stop buying books until I read the ones I have
3. Finish the first script - Gay John Wick
4. Don't buy any new shirts, all of 2023
5. Exercise more
6. Paint more
7. Skateboard more
8. ~~Publish Hearts & Farts on Father's Day~~
9. Publish the Rehab book on Nov 18th
10. Publish Sleeping 3
11. Be more patient (always)
12. Write sitcom script - Brooklyn to Boca

The Realization

The Eight Year Old:
Why are so many songs about losing your lover?

Me:
Because it happens to everybody, therefore it's a universal theme.

The Eight Year Old:
Will it happen to me?

Me:
😔 (realizing she has all her romantic heartbreaks still in her future, all of them)

Artiste peintre

Bad writer.
But can't turn it off.

Is there a word for that?
Maybe a French nouveau slang.

Maybe I will make up an expression.
Like Heidegger did.

Maybe I am a good writer.
Maybe not.

Doesn't really matter.
Not like I am going to stop.

dwy deglutition

the difference between dreams
coming true and jinxes
is a matter of semantics.

internally, you have to envision
that it will happen,
but don't externally mention
it has happened if the thing
you want has yet to happen.

you have to strike
without assumption;
wish with confidence,
before announcing with arrogance.

the difference between
realizing a dream
and ruining one
is simply shutting up
until it is real.

just as much as it matters
how much you put out into the world,
double your odds with how much
your withhold.

I was born a thief, I will die in Dada

not since Picasso's
"Portrait of Ambroise Villard"
have I been viscerally affected
by a work of art.

Basquiat's prolificness
takes the crown
(pun intended)

If I do end up
with a tombstone,
put the words on it:
"Wake up."

Living the Dream

I have to remind myself
that the "Dream" is not the end result.

The "Dream" is being
a wayward working writer,
and all that comes with that...

The rejections,
the shitty open mics,
writing drivel Black Friday email copy for money,
the constant internal debate,
the doubt, the fear, the love...

That is the "Dream,"
because once you've "made it"
you stop dreaming;
the minute you think you've achieved
the "Dream" is when you've lost sight of it.

The struggle is the dream.
The early mornings editing are the dream.
The sacrifices are the dream.

The nightmare of life
is actually the blessing
of living in pursuit of your passion.

Rork Toro

"No porter for me, perhaps next year"
is the best signify ever.

It's just me singing Papa Don't Preach
by Madonna by myself
in a high falsetto.

I give sadness a color, a shape,
tell it to take a hike tonight.

It's purple and the shape of shadow,
I can't do anything about it, because it's mine.

Life is a game with no flow,
except for what we remember.

We can't tell the future,
so we tell the past.

"As far back as I can remember,
I loved the movie GoodFellas,"
is how I start the film.

I am overwhelmed

In terms of archetypes,
I want to be the rebel
or the lover,
but I am most likely
the orphan,
with the goal to belong
despite cynical flaws.

I feel I am most authentic
when I am slightly tired,
in a goofy mood,
and a hoodie.

My freak flag
is a napkin,
covered in Chinese food.

Collecting flowers,
regarding existence,
while reading about
Eloise in the Plaza.

I am inactively always trying
to be a better person,
a different archetype,
less overwhelmed,
more the mood of entering
Disney World.

Everything we have seen,
everything we have done.

We are made by ourselves,

of ourselves,
and I get more knowledge (and hope)
from that fact.

The Epistemology of "Cheerios"
by Billy Collins

Pieces of time,
bowls of poetry.

every day, I stray
further from Hashem,
and deeper into Bushwick.

tying up loose ends,
resurrecting dead ends...

I live wherever I don't belong.

I am an open wound
of language...
to say so little hurts.

a kiss buried in the dark,
but the rest?
I ask as sunlight drips.

Pieces of poetry,
bowls of time.

Plantar Fasciitis: The Musical

Uniquely connecting the worlds of music, theatre and dance, Plantar Fasciitis: The Musical is a fresh exploration of the timeless tale of a young man's coming of old age told through the classic songs of music icon Annie Lennox and the bold visual imagination of legendary choreographer and theatre icon Twyla Tharp. The new musical is set within a low-rent traveling circus run by Captain A-a-ron, whose wagon hasn't moved from its location in some time — though not by lack of effort from his ragtag band of clowns and performers. One such performer is the animal trainer Cleo, a young woman exploited by Capt. A-a-ron and loved by his son, Coyote. Coyote longs for a world outside the confines of the family business, and as the circus show plays out, he must decide whether to flee or stay, and if he will listen to the podiatrist who tells him to get his first pair of ugly dad sneakers.

Jobbed by the Zebras

looking forward to leftover lasagna.
I'll watch the Magic game,
and put together a Barbie camper,
block out everyunimportthing.

It's overwhelming, the world.

There are so may books,
and WAY too much music,
not to mention
politics and economics,
tv shows and movies.

So.
Much.
Stuff.

Love and death,
rent and bills,
food and exercise.

Endless garbage,
and laundry,
and dishes.

What's not out of reach
is being a good dad
and a prolific poet.

And when life gives limes,
or when I am jobbed by zebras,
I can't offer much, besides "That sucks."

Because moving on doesn't come
without coping mechanisms.

And being present
is not accomplished
without ignoring the past
and the future.

To My Lenny

And the worlds you have yet to discover...

We are all born
to broken people
on their most honest
day of living.

You came to me, us,
like a peregrine,
and gave the glow of life,
and it has been my revenge
to care for you.

I waited to write this,
but I have been thinking
about these words
(for years) (five, six, eight),
since the morning you were born:

10:15am.

That Friday will always
LIVE
loud and strong,
the strongest and loudest,
like an anvil in my life of hammers
my silly life of poems
which was suddenly changed for the great,
because until then I assumed I was living,
but I wasn't.

When you breathed your first breath,
you gave me a light I had never known,

never seen, blinding & blessing.

You came out of the womb
with your eyes wide open,
and welcoming;
You wanted to see everything,
and you continue to want to see and know everything.

I love your questions,
and I want to give you a world of answers,
but I can't,
so keep asking.

That first night of nights,
I remember looking at you
like a lion,
and feeling like a protector
for the first time,
and the clock didn't matter anymore.

I will forever protect you.
I will forever love you.
Not to the matter of anything,
and that is a promise.

Just unconditional love.

I am excited
to teach you
how
to find laughter
in the middle of mayhem,
because you helped
me find solace.

Don't let these waves wash away your hopes,

in spite of life's lessons and treasons.
Life is good and fun and fun and good,
despite what I may say from time to time.

When you arrived,
you gave me arms,
and a reason to reach.

You looked at me and Mommy
with those big beautiful eyes,
and reassured both of us
that life is bigger than what we imagined,
and love is gigantic.

I couldn't wait to hold you and smell you
and introduce myself.
I'm your Dad
and
your entrance was magnificent
and
the most real moment of my existence.

You shattered my conception
of love, because...
You are my sky
and my reason why.

Even at my end,
I will take a time loop
to get back to you.

I'm crying while writing this,
and I am the luckiest person
in the wide world,
because of you.

Thank you for making me a Dad,
for helping me,
for opening my eyes.

Maybe you'll find books
of mine
when you are older;
That's the only voice I ever had
in this loud world,
except for telling you
to be brave and find love in everything.

Now go.
Do anything.

I love you.
The world I want to give you is **Love**.
Always. Try. To. Discover. Unconditional. Love.
And don't ever give up.

>Love,
>Forever,
>Your Dad
>
>>P.S.
>
>>Remember the 3 C's:
>>>Confidence
>>>Creativity
>>>Compassion

A poet rather than a criminal

Poetry, at its best,
like a life of crime,
is based on our mysterious variety
of forces.

From upbringing to outlook,
this is a combination of internal and external forces;
comedy and tragedy,
music and...well, poetry.

This is a variety embodied by great comics
like Buster Keaton, Margaret Cho,
the movie "Blazing Saddles,"
the poems of Emily Dickinson
and the writing of Mark Twain.

My hope is that the eccentricity,
many-centeredness and hierarchical excellence
of those cultural products will provide a model
that a poetic person can be proud of.

When a single word speaks volumes...
A devastating couplet is every poet's secret weapon;
just as a criminal has a knife or gun or crowbar.

Whether it's grumbling about having to go to bed
with nothing but a Sylvia Plath anthology for warmth
or crooning sweet nothings-that-are-actually-dark-somethings,
words bring clarity and drama, opening a secret passage
to someone's internal life
(just like a thief cracking open a safe).

Poem

I heard the term *Pachyderm*
a lot more when I was younger.
I thought I would encounter
more quicksand in life.

Humgleep

What is this person?
Anxious, excited, impatient.

Finding other words
in a word search
that are not on the list…
that is what life is all about.

Oscar Wilde famously wrote
in his 1889 Socratic dialogue format essay
'The Decay of Lying' that
"Life imitates art far more
than art imitates life."

And I have to disagree
when selfless love
is involved.

We are all works of art,
complicatedly imitating life.

(This whole book
is just trying to recreate
the feeling of life
and love.)

"Et al."

ASK. QUESTIONS.
Wanting to learn more is not foolish behavior.

Zoom out every once in a while
It's easy to get sucked into the day to day.
Flex your muscle of viewing the big picture:

+ What are you gaining from each experience?
+ How are you growing as a person?
+ Are there areas you aren't leaning into that you'd really like to?

And lastly, remember how unbelievably worthy you are.
It is vital for your growth to live and breathe your worth.

"I feel very lucky that I get to choose the things that are going to drive me crazy in life: that's writing and being a dad."

Ryan Buynak has been described as "the most prolific poet you've never heard of." He is a pugilist, punching poetry into existence as a battle against death. He has a baker's dozen books under his belt, and that is why he walks funny. A grateful father, Ryan is working on a novel, a screenplay, gluing old baseball cards to furniture found in the garbage, and anything else to avoid a real job. He is also the host of a fun, unique music podcast called Bothering the Band, in which he asks famous and emerging musicians super silly questions. You can find him by simply searching for Coyote Blood...on Google...not just, like, wandering the forest looking for actual blood from a coyote. Farts.